PRAISE FOR OWL MAGIC

A new title for a new moment. Combining the creative force of the feminine divine with the wisdom of the owl, this book guides you through the anxiety of the current moment. Owl Magic helps reclaim your intuitive power so you can build a better future from the position of your highest self.

— SHERIANNA BOYLE, AUTHOR OF EMOTIONAL DETOX FOR ANXIETY

Owl Magic takes you gently by the hand and leads you to deeper self-awareness and self-actualization through stories, myths, meditations, and writing prompts, inviting us to peel back the layers of who we are and how we navigate an imperfect world so we can step into our true power.

— RACHEL JEPSON WOLF, AUTHOR OF THE UNPLUGGED FAMILY ACTIVITY BOOK & HERBAL ADVENTURES

With bold insight and clear vision, Petiet illuminates the current crisis facing our world to offer a vision of hope and a path through trying times. Owl asks, Who will lead us? And the answer is us: You and me.

— LAURI ANN LUMBY, AUTHOR OF SONG OF THE BELOVED: THE GOSPEL ACCORDING TO MARY MAGDALENE

owl
magic

ALSO BY MARY PETIET

Minerva's Owls

Moon Tide: Cape Cod Poems

owl magic

Your Guide Through Challenging Times

MARY PETIET

Sea Crow Press
amplifying voices

For Will, who left too soon.

Once upon a time, when women were birds, there was the simple understanding that to sing at dawn and to sing at dusk was to heal the world through joy. The birds still remember what we have forgotten, that the world is meant to be celebrated.

— TERRY TEMPEST WILLIAMS, WHEN WOMEN WERE BIRDS:
FIFTY-FOUR VARIATIONS ON VOICE

CONTENTS

WELCOME TO OWL MAGIC

YOUR GUIDE THROUGH CHALLENGING TIMES

In this moment of boundless potential, connect to your highest self and your power of creative transformation. Transcend the anxiety of the current moment to lay the foundations for a better future.

We find ourselves in uncertain times, but times of high anxiety and unknown outcomes are also times of huge potential. Each seed we plant now will grow the future.

In these pages, you will find a toolbox of simple, anxiety-busting steps and exercises designed to connect you to your greatest potential and your highest self.

Drawing upon the transformative energy of the feminine divine, *Owl Magic* is an interactive guide to channeling your inner wisdom so you can achieve the greatest good for yourself and the changing world we live in.

The big question is: How will we manage it?

During the lockdown of spring 2020, I developed a series of steps to help me through this unprecedented moment. As my regular work writing promotional material dried up, I began to commit my evolving coping practices to paper. In time, *Owl Magic* became the book I needed to manage this moment, and I offer it here as a guide to help you.

Each practice in *Owl Magic* harnesses the energy of transformation to channel your inner wisdom.

The toolbox of simple steps includes guided meditations, yoga poses, universal laws, poetry, and writing/thinking prompts.

You need at least 20 minutes a day, a yoga mat, a notebook, and a comfortable pen.

I find I work best in isolation, but you are welcome to include friends, or even form a group if that is what calls.

There are no hard rules. Just give it time and space and honesty.

And see where it leads you.

1
OWL MAGIC

WISDOM AND CONNECTION

A Walker

*A walker
braved a blizzard's wake
and found a Snowy owl
frozen on the beach.*

*Too majestic to abandon,
she gathered it cold and lifeless
and wished it warm and quick.*

A taxidermist granted her whim.

*And ruffled white feathers became
forever smooth,
loose white wings
forever folded,
blind eyes forever keen,
the snowy owl
forever alive, but not.*

WHAT IS OWL MAGIC?

Owl Magic is inspired by the ancient power of the divine feminine to renew life. In this chapter, we journey back, without leaving our houses, to retrieve this powerful creative force that lies within us all. This vital force will fuel our growth as we rebuild ourselves and our world to meet these challenging times and build the future.

It's a strange time to be alive as we find ourselves between two eras. For many of us, the coronavirus stopped society and forced those of us lucky enough to have good health and safe homes inside, away from everything we knew and did in our normal routines. One way of life ended, and a new one began.

Such times of plague have historically led to times of change. As we stayed quietly at home to stop the spread of the virus, we began a new era—poised between the old world and ways of doing previously taken for granted, and the new world inevitably forming.

LET'S CALL THIS THE TIME BETWEEN.

As we navigate the shifting landscape of the Time Between, it is natural to feel a sense of loss and a loss of direction. When we do, we can call upon strong owl magic to guide our way.

Owls weave through the stages of life and many cultures, often as the embodiment of wisdom and the deepest soul level intuition. Owls are nocturnal with sharp eyes to pierce the dark, and legend places an owl upon Athena's shoulder to help her see the entire truth of a matter. Creatures of the night, owls are naturally connected to the moon and its cycles, and this links them to the feminine cycles of birth, growth, and death or maiden, mother, and crone.

Owl magic is a practice to access this wise intuition. Through a series of yoga poses, meditations, universal laws, and writing prompts, we can raise our magic to reach our highest selves and let our creativity flow as we follow the flights of this wise and mysterious creature.

There is magic you can find deep within yourself. As we experience the challenges of the Time Between, we can access this wisdom and creativity individually without having to leave the house. At the same time, we can harness this power to connect us to the ancient generations who knew it before us, to each other as we rediscover it, and to the future we are using it to create.

We can take some of the distance out of social distancing at a time when we most need human connection.

As the owl of wisdom soars past, she may drop a feather

Have you ever been outside and found a feather? Or perhaps many feathers? Feathers are signs of inspiration and connection to the muse close by.

Feathers are a sign of owl magic, and we often see them after a brush with mysticism. They symbolize wisdom attained, and as you start seeing them, you realize absolutely everything is connected, which leads us to our first universal law:

The Law of Connection: All things are connected and nothing happens in isolation.

The Law of Connection may sound obvious as you hear it, but it is something we need to remember. Once we remember our connection to things and each other, we begin to care, and once we care, our connections become sacred, and we protect where we may have previously destroyed. The Law of Connection means that what happens to others also happens to you.

Another name for it is Karma.

But what about the owls?

Once, God was a woman, and maybe, before that, women were birds.

The story of birds, women, owls, and ancient goddesses is old. Archaeologist and anthropologist Marija Gimbutas' research into Old Europe centers on the Danube region during the mysterious Neolithic past. Combining the evidence of pottery, sculpture, and mythology involving women, birds, the goddess, and the creative force, Gimbutas posits a peaceful goddess-oriented society poised between hunting-gathering and settled farming.

WAS GOD A WOMAN?

The Neolithic Great Mother appears carved in limestone tinted in ochre, the color of blood.

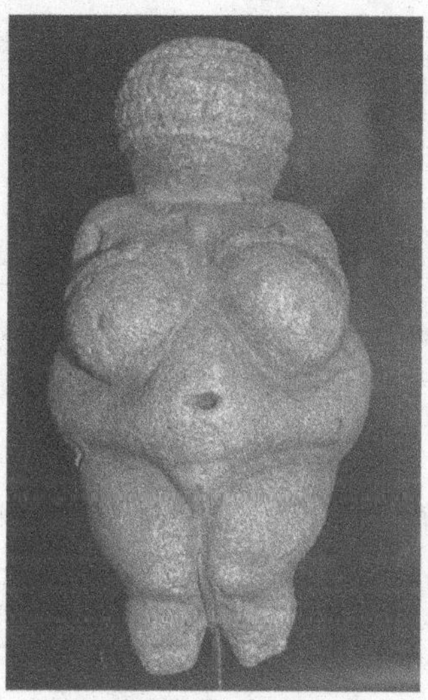

Venus of Willendorf photo by Don Hitchcock

Her births echo the Eastern idea of the births of successive universes and seasonal renewal of the fields, reproduction of livestock, and the experience of all mothers.

She is the life source, both giver and taker of life. She links us to the earth and the act of creation. When we revere her, we revere the earth.

When we create, we recall her creation.

The Great Mother brings us home.

Bird Goddesses from Gimbutas

These ancient figures have female bodies with the heads of birds.

Birds sing, so maybe this points to an ancient singing tradition, and birds lay eggs, which brings us back to procreation and the creative process, and finally, birds fly, inviting us to limitless horizons.

Owls are birds, too—it's all part of the connection

Later, Greek mythology associates the owl with Athena, the virgin goddess of wisdom. This Athenian coin depicts Athena on one side and a small owl with huge eyes outlined in what looks like an infinity symbol on the other.

Athenian coin showing Athena and her owl, c. 410 BCE

To the ancients, the term virgin meant independence, and Gimbutas linked the owl of Athena right back to the bird goddesses of ancient Europe.

The owl symbolizes wisdom, prophecy, and vision in many traditions worldwide and was adopted as a symbol of the city of Athens.

So let's get back to finding those feathers, we are going to create our owl magic

There are two common misconceptions most of us are probably familiar with. The first is the idea that wisdom only happens on the mountaintop. The second is that magic can only be attained by the initiated over long periods of study.

Both are untrue.

We are surrounded by magic. It is in the motes of dust drifting through the sunbeam across your desk. It is the sound of the wind, the waves, and the birdsong. It is the small hand reaching up to catch your own.

At the same time, wisdom permeates the patchwork moments of all our days as it weaves through the fabric of our busyness. It is available to each of us. The mountaintop is here. We simply need to notice it. Here is powerful owl magic, and we can use it to restore the life force of the feminine, harnessing it at this crucial time between times to create a new us in a new world.

THE YOGA POSE: OWL POSE

Owl Pose starts our sequence as a classic warm-up pose incorporating conscious breath and maybe just a little bit of shapeshifting.

Kneel on your favorite yoga mat with your legs folded and your weight resting on the back of your heels. Your spine is straight, and you are comfortable.

Owl Pose is inspired by owl vision. While owls see far in the dark, their eyes are fixed to their sockets, so they must move their heads to see.

Once you have settled on your yoga mat, begin to rotate your head like an owl might.

Gently move your head to the right and then around to the left. Move your head up and down. Roll your head clockwise and counterclockwise.

You are activating your owl vision.

Incorporate prana, the life force of conscious breath.

Breathing exercises are great stress busters. Once you've looked around with your owl eyes, find a fixed point to stare at and bring your palms to your knees. You are still resting on the back of your heels.

Breathe deeply and slowly. How does it feel? You are moving from your everyday breath, which might be quite shallow, to a deeper breathing experience. Observe the change as you deepen and lengthen your breath. You are connecting to your higher self. You are breathing yourself home.

THE MEDITATION

If you are comfortable kneeling, stay that way. If not, find a comfortable position on your yoga mat. Think of your yoga mat as a kind of flying carpet. You are going to be doing a lot of traveling from it.

Maintain the prana breath.

Imagine yourself connected to the center of the earth. Fill yourself with earth energy.

Now bring it up and out with your breath. Imagine you are flying on a warm breeze.

You have transitioned from finding feathers to having feathers.

The world below looks small, but you can see its connections. Viewed from above with owl eyes, everything is linked together.

Your owl vision is activating your third eye, you are going deep into Ajna, the Chakra of Light.

When your third eye opens, you may see an indigo or blue color behind the lids of your closed eyes.

When you are ready to land back on your mat, bring your hands to your armpits to make wings. Embrace your sillies here and flap your wings a bit as you land.

Writing Prompts

- Do you practice the Law of Connection? How has it changed you?

- What are the levels of your connection? Find your place in the wider web.

- What does it look like where you are? Can you draw or map it? Find your soul level mysticism, wisdom, and connection.

- Now that you have rooted solidly, what new ideas do you have? Record your wisdom and insight.

Fill your journal with your feathers.

Bonus ~ Wouldn't it be fun to try writing with a quill?

2
AS ABOVE, SO BELOW

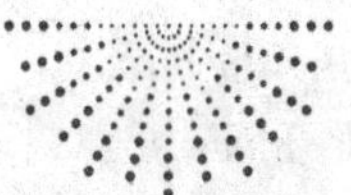

RETELL YOUR STORIES, CHANGE YOUR OUTCOME

We Remember, We Remake

Old flames
of burning times
are new friends
in these times,
warming us
joining us
connecting the circle
under the moon's
knowing light.

We remember
we remake
old ways
for a new world
As owl eyes scry burning embers
dragon-shaped
flame-spewing
emissaries of the old goddess.

How deep is owl vision?

Owl vision looks through and beyond any situation or story. With owl vision, you can see above and below, within and without. This means the cosmos above reflects the earth below, while the mind within reflects practical happenings without.

Using owl vision to see through your stories

Do you tell yourself the same stories over and over and end up with the same results? Is it possible the entire world is doing the same thing as the news becomes more and more extreme? We cannot fix the planet right here right now, but we can look around ourselves and make as much right as possible.

One powerful way to do this involves considering our stories and possibly changing them to achieve a better outcome.

Once I thought I would never find a parking space for my car. I drove around and around the parking lot, telling myself I would never find a spot. Then I remembered something I had read recently, about imagining what you need in order to manifest it.

So I changed my story

I crossed my fingers and visualized myself finding a perfect parking spot, close to the store, easy to get into, just right.

I did another circle back around the parking lot, and not one, but four spots had opened up!

In changing my story from 'there are no parking spots' to 'there is a perfect spot here for me,' I had changed my energetic vibration to match what I wanted. And there it was:

The Law of Attraction: Like attracts like.

What we put out is what we get back. We can apply this to our smallest stories, like parking the car, and we can apply it to our biggest cultural constructs as well.

We can even go back to the beginning and retell the story of Eve.

The traditional story, according to the book of Genesis in the Bible, places Eve with Adam in the Garden of Eden. Everything is perfect, and the only rule they have to follow is not to eat the fruit of the Tree of Knowledge of Good and Evil.

But Eve is charmed by the serpent into eating the fruit, and she offers it to Adam, and God expels them both from the Garden of Eden as punishment. Eve takes full blame for the original sin of eating the apple and the subsequent expulsion from Eden. Through Eve, all women have carried the blame ever since.

Just as driving around a parking lot thinking 'I'll never find a space' led to my never finding a space, this story of Eve's blame, and by extension that of all women, has led to the degeneration of the feminine life-giving principle throughout most of recorded history.

Maybe Eve's story is really about how women's lives changed from the powerful givers of life in the goddess-oriented societies of Old Europe Gimbutas describes, to second-class lives in later societies, where their capacity for creation of life and art was stifled.

Eve's story has been an excuse to treat women as *less,* and it underpins the social structures of patriarchy and capitalism that are now, especially in the Time Between, showing their dysfunction as they fail to stop climate change, fail to build equitable societies, fail to protect their weakest members, and lead to pandemic through unbalancing the natural world. They are failing to embrace the life-giving principle subjugated by the story of Eve.

But if we retell the story with our owl vision, Eve becomes a hero, and we change the energetic output to get a different result.Maybe Eve's choice to gain knowledge by eating the fruit was an exercise of free will which came at a high price. She was curious about the worldly and the earthly, the human concerns, joys, and pain that we must all share.

Maybe she decided to grow up, and as she ate the apple, she accepted knowledge with the power it brought and the joys and pain it implied.

In this story, Eve casts us from the garden, but she gives us our humanity.

Stepping back even further, Lilith, the first wife of Adam, would appreciate this retelling.

Legend has it Lilith left the Garden of Eden in the days before Eve for refusing to become subservient to Adam.

Researchers speculate Lilith may have been based on the Babylonian goddess Lilitu.

Here she is.

Does the Burney Relief from Babylon depict Lilith?

You knew she would have wings and bird feet and be flanked by owls, right?

THAT'S SOME POWERFUL OWL MAGIC TO CALL IN

Sometimes we need to change our own stories, as we have changed Eve's and Lilith changed hers.

Imagine what would happen if the world embraced Eve as the hero who handed us our humanity. It would put out the energy that affirms life, which would bring back affirmation of the life force and creation embodied by the feminine. It could stop wars, preserve habitats, and endorse green energy. It could improve the situation of millions.

On a smaller scale, embracing Eve's new story personally can change your own story.

You can imagine women as curious creators, innovators ahead of their time. As the world changes quickly in the Time Between, you can imagine yourself as part of the change and rebuilding we are going to face in the wake of the pandemic.

You can raise your energetic vibration to match what you desire and make it so.

THE YOGA POSE: MOUNTAIN POSE

Yoga practice consists of a series of poses designed to stretch your muscles while relaxing your body to the point that your mind can stretch itself. Each pose evokes something significant.

To ground yourself, assume Mountain Pose. Stand with your feet at hip-width. Spread your toes and feel your feet interact with the ground. Stand tall and straight and grow from your waist. Breathe. Establish a solid foothold. You are connected to the earth as a strong mountain is connected to the earth. Breathe and receive energy from the earth.

Incorporate prana, the life force of conscious breath.

Breathe deeply with intention. In and out. Take stock of how you feel at this moment. Breathe into places that need it, for example, if you are feeling sad, breathe into your heart chakra.

THE MEDITATION

Maintain the breath. Ease into a comfortable position from Mountain Pose, seated, or maybe on your back. You will stay rooted.

You are on a journey alone, and you are approaching a mountain. You have left the company of others because it does not suit you and you feel your gifts are undervalued.

The closer you get to the mountain, the bigger the mountain gets. It is huge. You circle it, probing for a way in. There, you see the entrance. It is dark and a little scary, but you go in slowly and find a path to follow.

You go deeper and deeper and deeper into the mountain. It gets darker and darker and darker. In your head, you are repeating your story about not fitting in, the story of why you left in the first place.

Then you see light ahead. You follow it. Deep in the center of the mountain, you find a chamber with a low fire burning in a hearth. It is warm and you see no one there. You sit to rest and stare at the flames.

You are sleepy, but not too sleepy to notice the flames are arranging themselves into pictures. Your owl vision is kicking in here.

You see your home and how it looks without you. You see an empty space there, space you used to fill.

You see all of the empty spaces that would be left if all of the world's women vanished.

Then you see a crack in the way things are, and beyond it, you see a new world.

In this world, your space and all the other spaces are filled again, and women are valued and creating.

This is the world we can build together if we change our stories by embracing the feminine life force.

You are ready to go back and tell a new story.

You follow a new path out of the mountain. You thank the mountain for its wisdom and find your way back to your place as co-creator of a new story in a new world.

Writing Prompts

- What does *as above, so below* mean to you?

- How can you practice the Law of Attraction?

- What kind of energy are you putting out?

- What are you attracting?

- Retell your most important stories.

3

ALL SHALL BE WELL

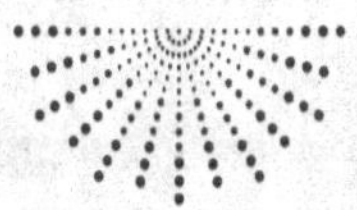

TRANSFORM THROUGH TURMOIL

Leap into the Song

When worldly news
hangs heavy
burdensome and raw,
leap
into a joyful lifesong
with the wind and crows and gulls.

Gliding, swooping, calling,
soft song
or loud song,
moving
through it all
swirling
linking light.

Leap
into the song.

Owl Wisdom

The current pandemic is not the first pandemic and now is not the first Time Between. The past is certainly no stranger to tragic life-altering situations involving mass suffering and social upheaval. We are in such a time now, compounded by ongoing global crises, including climate change, inequality, and unfair distribution of resources.

We find ourselves living in uncertain times

In Europe, the end of the fourteenth century was also a harrowing time. One-third of the population died of bubonic plague as the Hundred Years War raged and the church split between rival popes.

Like today, the structures people assumed were permanent began to vanish. And like today, a certain kind of wisdom helped people survive the uncertainty.

Think of it as Owl Wisdom

Owls have a quiet about them, allowing them to observe and notice. They embody an independence that lets them forge ahead with the vision to see the way. They occupy the moment and work with what they have. They soar above the fray.

Here is the owl wisdom you can apply to your situation, the same wisdom women mystics of earlier times tapped into as their worlds convulsed.

In the late fourteenth century, one mystic found peace in the storm by finding a connection to a loving God through something she called Body Prayer. Her name was Julian of Norwich, and what she called Body Prayer looks a lot like modern yoga.

It is also full of owl wisdom

All shall be well, and all shall be well, and all manner of thing shall be well. ~Julian of Norwich

As an anchorite at the church of St. Julian in Norwich, England, Julian of Norwich would have been at home with the idea of social isolation. An anchorite chooses a solitary life to cultivate internal focus.

Julian of Norwich, Stained Glass Window from St. Julian's Church, Norwich, photo by Evelyn Simak

Quarantine? No problem

Her real name is lost to the ages, but it is almost certain she lost her husband and children to the plague and nearly died of it herself. While ill, she experienced a series of visions about the nature of love, which redefined her connection to God and faith in goodness through awful times.

She described her experience in the first known book in English written by a woman. It was called *Revelations of Divine Love*.

Notes on the nature of God and love

The god Julian of Norwich encountered is the traditional Christian god. What is different is how she approached him through the divine feminine.

If you think of the many faces of God, any one of those faces might appeal to you individually. Or maybe none of them appeal. Maybe what you find is your highest self. Either way, the message of universal love and connection is as powerful now as it was in earlier times.

Jesus Christ ...is our true mother; we derive our being from him—and this is the foundation of motherhood... For just as truly as God is our father, so too God is our mother. ~Julian of Norwich

She was surprisingly modern. As her contemporaries worshipped a harsh patriarchal god, Julian of Norwich called in a radically feminine deity that added motherhood and love to the equation. Her god was both father and mother, and, as the transcendentalists would centuries later, she saw God in everything as she declared salvation universal.

She shares a vision of infinity as a tiny thing the size of a hazelnut and tells us she has held this tiny thing in her hand:

I looked at this with the eye of my soul and thought, 'What is this?' And this is the answer that came to me, 'It is all that is made.' I saw that this tiny thing had three properties that were essential to it. The first is that God made it; the second is that God loves it; the third that God preserves it. I was astonished that it managed to survive: it was so small I thought that it might disintegrate. And in my mind, I heard this answer: 'It lives on and will live on forever because God loves it.' So everything owes its existence to the love of God. ~Julian of Norwich

Here is an expression of our next law straight out of an earlier time of pandemic and social upheaval:

The Universal Law of Love: The force that binds everything together.

It is not romantic love. It is the energy behind the Law of Connection. It is unconditional and all accepting. It is the opposite of fear.

Think of it like gravity.

It is the glue that can hold us together, individually and collectively, through tumultuous times.

Every situation presents a choice of action. Imagine what happened when Julian of Norwich's life was derailed by bubonic plague. In no time at all, she lost her family and all the trappings of active, worldly life in medieval Norwich.

She could easily have reverted to fear, the opposite of love, and simply ceased to be.

What sustained her in her Time Between? Love.

Our lives have also changed rapidly.

Within one week, most of us found ourselves in a state of lockdown due to the coronavirus. It was a scene repeated all over the planet. Maybe some of us have been sick or lost loved ones.

Some of us are sheltering in place comfortably. Some of us are suffering, some of us are dying, and some of us are leaving quarantine and picking up the pieces in a changed world roiling with political instability.

For all of us, the futures we planned are uncertain.

What can sustain us in our Time Between? Love.

PRACTICING LOVE IN THE CHALLENGING TIME BETWEEN

Julian of Norwich would have recognized this well-known verse from 1 Corinthians 13:4-6:

> *Love is patient, love is kind. It does not envy, it does not boast, it is not proud. It is not rude, it is not self-seeking, it is not easily angered, it keeps no record of wrongs. Love does not delight in evil but rejoices with the truth.*

It is that simple. And that hard, as well. The practice of love shows in our actions.

Love is patient.

Be patient with yourself. You do not need to be wildly productive right now despite what you see online. Self-love is crucial, especially now, so you can love others in turn. Be patient with others, and be patient with yourself. We are all finding our way in a new reality.

Love is kind.

Kindness holds hands with patience at this point. Have you checked in with yourself and your needs? Have you thought of the needs of those around you? Can you help your neighbors?

Love does not envy or boast.

Are you safe right now? Hold quiet gratitude for all the good things.

It is not rude, it is not self-seeking.

Compassion and regard for the people you are closest to makes a huge difference in normal life but are especially important in uncertain times.

It is not easily angered, it keeps no record of wrongs.

Back to patience, the faith and will to persevere. Can you diffuse anger with kindness and empathy? Let past wrongs go, and focus on future goodness.

Love does not delight in evil but rejoices with the truth.

This one seems especially important right now. So much truth is coming to light. As we self isolate, we are finding time to examine our truths, and while the situation outside deteriorates, we are seeing the honest underbelly of the structures we till recently took for granted. Do we need to destroy the planet to maintain a non-sustainable lifestyle? If we can stop the world for a virus, can we not make the changes we need to stop climate change? Post-pandemic, we ask ourselves if we have violated our place in the web of life, and how to reintegrate ourselves within it so we and it can flourish.

Let's swoop in owl-wise and explore how Julian of Norwich invented yoga in fourteenth-century England. Yoga is more than physical activity, it is also a form of intense meditation designed to link you to your highest self.

In Sanskrit, the word *yoga* means *to yoke with the divine.*

This is what Julian of Norwich was doing through her series of poses she called Body Prayer. It is strongly reminiscent of a sun salutation.

Through this meditative exercise, Julian of Norwich found love instead of fear in a society shocked by pandemic and uncertainty and war.

Our society is suffering similar shock, with a climate crisis thrown in for good measure.

WE CAN TURN TO LOVE INSTEAD OF FEAR THROUGH THE PRACTICE OF BODY PRAYER

Body Prayer provides the firm grounding that links us to the highest energy of love. Remember the power of love and transformation. When the bubonic plague of Julian of Norwich's era ended, the path was clear for the Renaissance. As you explore the following poses and meditation, find the calm and potential within the storm where love resides. Then, because everything is connected, you can bring it back to share with others.

THE POSE & THE MEDITATION: BODY PRAYER

Stand firmly on your yoga mat. Body Prayer consists of a series of four standing poses. First, initiate your prana breath, breathe deeply, in and out. Then shift your focus.

- **Await** – the posture of receiving. Hold your hands open at waist level. You are welcoming the presence of God or your highest self.

- **Allow** – this is the posture of opening. Reach up with your hands open to welcome the coming of God's presence or the presence of your own highest self.

- **Accept** – the posture of taking. Cup your hands at your heart and take in whatever comes.

- **Attend** – this is the posture of willingness to act on what has been given. Extend your hands with palms open.

Await, allow, accept, attend.

Repeat the sequence while maintaining the breath.

Writing Prompts

- How has your life changed recently?

- Write a note to future generations explaining what is happening in our world now.

- If you imagine a divine presence, what form does it take?

- How do you practice love of self and others?

- What is the most loving thing you have witnessed?

4

TREE MAGIC

ASSUME ABUNDANCE

Old Oak Tree

Oak Tree
knows why
growing into the wind
is certainly no solution.

It tried once,
and proof
of the attempt
still lingers
in the gnarled trunk
forced northward
by a strong south wind.

Oak Tree
stands among the oak trees.
Screech owls shriek there,
reminding us
to bend with the wind.

GO HUG A TREE!

The Japanese have a beautiful tradition called forest bathing that takes you outside to surrender to the balm of the forest. If you can, go out among the trees and listen. If you are in quarantine, try your backyard, or your window. Inside, you might sit with a houseplant.

CONJURE THE TREES AND LISTEN

Join Owl on a high tree branch to see far and wide. Listen quietly to the trees. You might be surprised by what you hear.

Trees are in constant conversation, and you are welcome to join. Their topic might depend on the season or the weather. They may be dancing in an early March gale or murmuring with new leaves on a soft summer breeze. They might be whistling bare in a winter gale, or quietly sighing in fall's mellow light.

The trees are our ancient companions.

If you close your eyes and listen, they have stories to tell.

TREES LIVE BY THE UNIVERSAL LAW OF CONNECTION

When you step into a forest or a stand of trees, picture their underground root systems the same size as their leaf canopy. Each individual root system is connected to the ones next to it, creating a kind of tree internet as they communicate along their connected roots. When one tree dies, it uses these channels to send its remaining resources out to benefit the surviving community.

Trees live in a nurturing collective, so while we hear the murmuring of leaves above, a profound conversation is ongoing through the roots below.

TREES OF LIFE

The Tree of Knowledge and the Tree of Life were not exclusive to the Garden of Eden. Tree symbolism occurs many times in many cultures around the world.

In Norse legend, the great tree of life, Yggdrasil, links the worlds above and below, and at its base sit the three Norns recording human lives and deciding human fates. Before Christ was nailed to a tree, Odin sacrificed himself on Yggdrasil in a bid to gain knowledge of everything. Throughout the ancient Middle East, to the Far East, to pre-Columbian America, trees appear as images of life, connecting the earth and the sky.

As above, so below.

Trees are connected givers, and they have given us everything—from a cosmic structure to the houses we live in, the furniture we sit on, the tools we build with, and the air we breathe.

Are you sitting on a wooden chair in a wooden house? That wood was once a tree. Without trees, we stop breathing. We depend on what trees give to live. So do other species, including the screech owl, who nests in cozy tree hollows.

Conjure the trees

You are entering a network of reciprocity where it is assumed there is always enough to go around and where resources are sent where they are needed when they are required, which leads us to our next universal law:

The Law of Giving and Receiving: Universal energy flows between two points to make giving and receiving a constant energetic exchange. In short: Give and you shall receive.

Think of it as a different aspect of the Law of Attraction.

Ditch the scarcity mentality

The best thing we can do is ditch the concept of scarcity. Scarcity is the fear of too little. If you apply this fear to yourself, you set yourself up to experience it because you are sending out the energy that calls scarcity back to you.

The people hoarding toilet paper in the pandemic are ensuring that there will not be enough toilet paper to go around. The roots of hoarding lie in fear of scarcity.

Remember the character Scrooge in *A Christmas Carol* by Charles Dickens? The story of the miserly Ebenezer Scrooge is the perfect example of scarcity at work. Scrooge lived in a time of inequity, not unlike our own, and he hoarded resources that others needed, specifically the family of his clerk, Bob Cratchit. The Cratchit family was poor but happy, while Scrooge, who had everything, was a miserable character indeed.

Remember those trees sending resources where and when they are needed?

That is what Scrooge had to do to find happiness. It took the visit of three ghosts on a long Christmas Eve to sway him to finally ditch the scarcity mentality, and when he did, by sharing with the Cratchit family, his life changed for the better. Sharing made him happy.

IF YOU MAKE GENEROSITY A PRACTICE, IT WILL COME BACK TO YOU THREEFOLD

Consider witches, some of whom live by the threefold law of return, which states that the energy you put out will be returned to you three times over. Your thoughts and words form your intentions and actions, which is why the act of creating words is called spelling. A cast spell is energy in motion, and quickly assumes its own life.

The Giving Tree by Shel Silverstein is a story about what happens when the giving, or the energetic exchange, is one-sided. The story is about the relationship between a boy and a female apple tree. In the beginning, the boy visits the tree, and they are friends. The tree gives the boy gifts throughout his life, among them apples to sell so he can have money and wood to build a house and a boat until finally, the tree is but a stump, and the boy an old man. The tree has been happy to give unconditionally, and the boy has never thanked her.

It is a profoundly disturbing story, as it violates the universal Law of Giving and Receiving.

For the course of his entire life, the boy simply takes from the tree until there is nothing left. The tree says she is happy that he is happy, but the energy is one-sided, and the flow of return has stopped. It is easy to see the human species in the boy, and the planet in the tree as we continue to take as much as we can until there is nothing left of nature and we have destroyed it.

That stagnant energy might have a lot to do with how we ended up where we are: in unequal societies, on a planet with quickly dwindling resources, in the middle of a pandemic.

WE NEED TO RESTORE THE FLOW OF ENERGY ON EVERY LEVEL TO HEAL NATURE AND OURSELVES

Use your owl vision to look through and beyond. If maybe we once were birds, we might imagine what it would be like to live like the trees.

Consider the internet as our version of the trees' root system. It connects and allows us to communicate similarly. We have the technology to restore the energetic flow, which would ensure an equitable society.

Right now, I am writing from lockdown. It is week six. I live near an almost empty nature reserve, so I am lucky I can go out amongst the trees while maintaining social distance.

In the last six weeks, the air has become amazingly crisp and clean. I can taste its sweetness. I have never experienced such a thing before, and I imagine this experience is happening in many other places.

Now is a great moment to be a tree for the air alone.

When we went into lockdown and stopped spewing pollution, we stopped getting polluted air back.

This Time Between is the bridge to the Time After, and we are crossing the bridge now. In the Time After, will we simply resume our destructive behavior, or will we remember the clean air and protect it?

PRACTICING THE UNIVERSAL LAW OF GIVING AND RECEIVING WHILE TIMES ARE UNCERTAIN

The Universal Law of Giving and Receiving has the potential to restructure society along equitable lines if it can be embraced politically by the majority. In the meantime, we can learn from the trees about how to incorporate it into our own lives, and we can hope the change will come literally from the ground up.

Practicing this law is really about always contributing something. It does not have to be big or expensive, it just needs to keep the energy of give and take in continuous motion to ensure resources keep moving where they need to go.

- Practice generosity with the assumption that there is enough. Leave a tip if you can, and pay the coffee ahead.

- Give a smile, and you will get one back.

- Reach out. Especially if you are in quarantine, or a friend is. Check in with each other.

- Give the smallest of gifts: a flower, a shell, freshly baked bread.

- Give the gift of your time to a good cause.

- Give with love, and give with free abandon.

THE YOGA POSE: TREE POSE

Make your way to your yoga mat.

Tree Pose builds upon the same grounding as Mountain Pose and activates the root chakra, Muladhara. Muladhara is concerned with our most basic wants and security.

In Tree Pose, you are rooting yourself tree-like to the earth.

Engage your prana breath. Breathe deeply of the fresh air. Slowly in to your belly and back, then out.

To start, stand on your yoga mat with your feet at hip-width. Now feel the ground beneath you. Next, stretch your feet and plant them on the ground intentionally. Reach your roots down deep into the center of the earth and bring up the energy.

Connect to the energy.

Shift your weight to one side, into your left leg. Feel that shift. Then bring your right foot to your left ankle, and slowly move your right foot up your left leg while bending the right leg at the knee. Your balance is between the right foot pushing into the left leg, which pushes back.

You are stable. You are growing roots into the earth while supporting yourself in the atmosphere. Your lower half is solidly grounded below you, allowing you to wave your hands gently above your head as branches in the breeze. Feel the energy from deep in the earth moving through you and out from your branches, raising the collective energy. You are a conduit.

Remember, there is enough energy for you and the collective. By giving energy, you receive energy.

Breathe into it. You are of the earth, and you are of the air, and you cannot break because you can bend.

You are strong.

READY TO DANCE IN THE SACRED GROVE?

Once, when we might have been birds, we learned, played, and worshipped in sacred groves. The ancient Greek Platonic Academy graced a grove of oaks sacred to Athena and known to house the little owls associated with her. The oak grove was also sacred to the Druids, who held their ceremonies outside within the trees and personified summer as the Oak King and winter as the Holly King.

You can still find trees decorated with offerings in rural Scotland as people leave them gifts in exchange for an answer to their prayers.

Even two thousand years of Christianly have not eradicated the ancient power of trees.

THE MEDITATION

First, make yourself comfortable and quiet.

We are becoming birds. Put on your owl wings and fly with me.

We are coming in low over the North Sea to the east coast of Scotland. A long sandy beach stretches out before us, a ribbon between land and sea. The air is cool and tinged with sea-brine, and the waves are crashing in below.

Ruined cathedral walls stand gaunt on the headland in the light of a full August moon as we glide overhead, leaving the ancient town of St. Andrews behind. We are following the road to Dunino.

Feel the wind through your feathers, and feel your wings glide on the air currents.

The land is dark below as you follow the narrow farm track to a lonely parish church.

From the sky, you can see where the stones stood in a circle. The modern church stands within the old stone circle. Many of the ancient stones are today incorporated in the church walls.

Effectively the circle still stands.

You circle it three times, flying slowly.

Then you fly over the woods behind the church. There are lights among the trees. You smell fresh water and woodsmoke. You see a circle of women among the trees on the rocks above the burn that marks the sacred well.

You circle it three times, flying slowly.

You land gracefully and shape-shift back into a woman.

You walk the circumference of the circle three times and join the circle at its easternmost point.

You have joined the circle of sisters who keep the ancient day of Lughnasadh (pronounced LOO-nə-sə).

The circle blesses the land for the yearly food and grain of the harvest. It is a circle of thanksgiving, a blessing of gratitude upon the land to ensure this yearly harvest and the harvests of the future.

There is a sister at each compass point of the circle.

The sister on the Western point calls out to the sunset, the ending of things, the path into the Western sun the dead must travel.

The sister on the Northern point calls out to the cold, to winter, to the death, the barren fields, and stillness.

The sister of the Southern point calls out to the summer sun, warmth, fullness and life, long twilights, and fields of ripening grain.

At the Eastern point of the circle, you call in the sunrise, birth, and potential for good.

As one, the circle raises their lamps and walks three times around.

The perambulation ends, and an intention is set.

All good things are to be received in gratitude, that the flow of energy is maintained through reciprocity.

To receive, you must give.

Each sister leaves a trinket in the foot-shaped pool above the burn.

Each sister is acting as a creator of bounty.

You leave a beautiful shell from your favorite beach, an offering to the strong goddess who guards this sacred site where kings have been crowned and the harvest ensured since time immemorial.

A shooting star streaks across the sky, and the circle unweaves.

Each sister puts her owl wings back on, and, a bird once more, you fly in the light of the sinking moon, past the cathedral walls, over the beach.

Follow the path of the moon back to your yoga mat.

Circle the periphery of the mat three times before you land.

Writing Prompts

- What is the hardest gift you have ever given? Why?

- What generous impulses have you received?

- What would a reciprocal world look like?

- What are our obligations to each other?

5

APOCALYPSE

FACE YOUR FEAR

Imagine

Imagine
the air stays clean
imagine
the grief is gone
imagine
the ocean clean
imagine
the people together.

Imagine
the planet healed
imagine
the people healed
imagine
the fear is gone.

Imagine the poets were right
and this is the moment we changed.

Apocalyptic vision

Have you ever imagined soulless zombie armies, mushroom clouds, alien invasion, and of course, pandemic? We have read about the apocalypse in novels and watched it over and over again on movie screens. We have imagined dystopia and a violent, imminent end to everything we know, and we have probably imagined ourselves amongst the survivors, because who wants to contemplate their own mortality?

These are modern apocalyptic visions. They are rooted in fear, and they always happen to someone else. Except now, perhaps.

The fictional pandemic has suddenly become real, and the political instability is happening to all of us in some way, right now. If we are lucky, we get to sit it out on the couch in our yoga pants. If we are not lucky, we may have been sick, or someone we love may have been sick, or maybe we have to leave the couch because our jobs are essential. We may also be out risking danger to protest for a better world.

It is happening to all of us, and while we are probably all scared and thinking apocalyptic thoughts, we are also experiencing the current moment in very different ways.

It turns out it is not zombies or aliens or nuclear war. It is a virus, a microscopic enemy we cannot even see. It is social upheaval, dredging up all of the dark aspects of this world we need to fix, and it looks like it might have to get worse before it gets better.

Open your owl eyes

Expand your owl vision. Owls always see the truth and are comfortable flying through dark shadows. Summon your owls. Athena is a battle goddess, and the owl at her shoulder protects her in dark places.

THIS IS NOT THE FIRST APOCALYPSE

It has happened many times before, and it is possible to think of apocalypse as more of an ongoing situation than a one-time event. Every time a species goes extinct, they have had their apocalypse. Every time a habitat is destroyed, it is an apocalypse, and the thing most apocalypses have in common is that they are generally man-made.

ARE WE THE APOCALYPSE?

Did the virus jump species to humans because we put so much pressure on the natural environment? Maybe. And is it the nature of the virus to invade a host and drain it until it is exhausted in the same way humans invade the land and drain it until it too is exhausted? Possibly.

While pop culture defines apocalypse as the kind of explosive world-ending event we have seen in the movies, people have, in fact, been predicting the end of the world pretty much forever.

And in some times and places, it did end. But never for long, and often not at all.

Notice the fear behind the apocalyptic vision.

Apocalyptic predictions generally follow times of disruption or uncertainty, often involving war, plague, or the sighting of comets in the sky.

One of the earliest apocalyptic predictions was made in ancient Judea by the Essenes, who thought their battle with Rome was the end battle. For them, it was the end, but it was not the end for everyone.

The world has been predicted to end by antichrist, fire, and flood at different times by different people—yet still, we are here.

Between 1290 and 1335, Joachim of Fiore predicted the end of the world twice. His second prediction was a rescheduling of the first after it failed to materialize, and that was followed by the Black Death, which many considered the real end times.

Cotton Mather predicted the end of the world three times, and Nostradamus was specific in his prediction of July 1999.

We all remember the Y2K predictions and the Mayan Doomsday of 2012.

How many times and ways might the world have ended?

Bad things have happened, bad things are happening now, but the world has not ended yet, and neither have we.

Every previous apocalypse has been based on a false fear.

We are living in our own apocalyptic Between Times, which brings us to our next universal law:

The Universal Law of Courage: Own your fear and face it down through direct action.

This is how to make your fear a constructive agent of change in a rapidly changing world.

Let's take another look at the apocalypse through our owl eyes

According to the Oxford English Dictionary, the word apocalypse comes from the Greek *apokalupt,* which means to uncover or reveal.

What is being revealed right now in this Time Between?

Maybe instead of a spectacular end to civilization, we are living through a time of painful, difficult change, in which everything we need to fix personally, locally, and globally, is being revealed.

This is the reset button

As we stay inside to protect each other from infection, outside the planet is healing, and we are learning the changes we thought were impossible to make are, in fact, possible.

Remember, the Black Death was an apocalyptic Time Between which led to the Renaissance. Let's fly through the darkness of revelation on our owl wings. Let's mitigate some of the fear brought on by the situation by looking straight through it to the other side.

The Middle Ages counted on God to establish peaceful conditions, the Enlightenment thought reason was the solution, and now, today's world calls for another route forward.

Owl asks, 'Who?' And the answer is us: you and me

We are the route to the other side. Our actions now can take us out of fear and into courage, moving us and the collective through the Time Between into the Time After.

Face your fear and act.

It is a tall order.

Call in the Universal Law of Love while you are at it because love is the opposite of fear.

Start small and personal

Recently I noticed wrinkles and gray hair appearing. We live in a society that values youth over all else, but my body was changing. At first I was horrified because, for years, I thought it would never happen to me. But it did, and it was awful—until I considered the crone aspect of the threefold goddess: from maiden to mother to crone.

I looked the crone in the eye and saw she was wise.

Crone is an uncovering and revealing of the final stage of wisdom and calm, and it is a privilege to achieve it. I am by no means there yet, but I have become comfortable with the journey.

This leads to a wider net, the fear of death

Death might be the ultimate uncovering and revelation, I do not know for sure because I am not dead, but perhaps our fear of other things is under-pinned by our fear of death. If we can manage our fear of death, maybe we can lessen our other fears.

It is perfectly reasonable in a pandemic to fear death. While the owls of wisdom certainly flank the crone's shoulders, owls are also associated with death.

The banshee's shriek and the owl's screech might be one.

Most of us have not seen death upfront because it has become so sanitized. We have little direct experience with it, so it remains mysterious. But as the only species with self-awareness, we are certainly aware of our mortality.

Let healthy fear serve a purpose

There is a reason for fear. It governs the fight or flight impulse, which can save your life. Imagine you are an ancient human on the savannah and you see a hunting lion. Fear is what will propel you away from the predator and out of danger. Fear can be your track to safety.

Unhealthy fear is the fear that paralyzes us

Fear of not being enough undermines your best efforts and leads only to failure.

Fear of scarcity leads to real scarcity as resources dwindle, as seen in pandemic panic shopping.

Fear of change leads to stagnation.

Fear of death leads to a fear of living.

The Universal Law of Courage is about staring each of these fears in the face and moving through them.

What if we accept death as something as natural as birth, making it a natural experience instead of a scary one. From darkness comes light, and from death comes new life and innovation.

We can take our own lives in hand and live each moment to its fullest, so in the end, we are replete.

That clears the way for you to face all the other fears that spring from death, which are probably coming up now under pandemic pressure.

What if we follow Ram Dass and agree to walk each other home?

Practicing courage in challenging times

When you practice courage, you are making space for the positive attributes that follow it. Owl vision can help you face your fears so you can move forward.

Courage leads to honesty, empathy, kindness, and the conviction you need to live your best life.

You know you are practicing courage when you feel a nervous flutter in your stomach. Courage is not easy. It demands our best.

- Take responsibility for yourself.

- Own your actions. All of them.

- Dare to do it. Take the risk, start new things.

- Be yourself.

- Commit to your choices.

- Pay attention.

- Accept failures and learn from them.

Courage is what we need to rebuild ourselves and our world in the wake of the pandemic, and courage is how we are going to move forward.

Practicing courage will help you navigate the difficult times.

Three steps to managing fear through challenging times:

Stage One: Hoarding

Brought about by sudden frightening changes to daily life.

- This is when all the toilet paper disappears from the stores and other shelves are emptied as people panic buy. This is a control mechanism.

- You find yourself in a negative zone brought on by obsession with the news, and you take on the negativity and pass it forward.

Stage Two: Adjustment and Acknowledgement

Accepting the new situation.

- Now you can look straight at it. Face it. How does it feel? If you cannot control it, drop it.

- Trade in the negativity of constant news coverage for something positive. No wonder baking is popular in a crisis!

- Look for the best in everyone. We are all finding our way in a new world.

Stage Three: Action

Giving your best to the current moment.

- Transmute fear through direct action.

- What is right in front of you that you can do now?

- Find a purpose you can align with your talents, adapt to the present and work for a better future.

THE YOGA POSE: WARRIOR POSE

There are three stages to Warrior Pose. This is Warrior One. This pose helps open your third chakra, the Manipura. Located in your solar plexus, the Manipura is the home of courage.

If you feel frightened, intimidated, inadequate, or victimized, it may be a sign your Manipura is blocked. Opening your Manipura is a great way to tap into the courage that is already there waiting for you.

Stand on your yoga mat and engage your prana breath. Find a fixed point in the room to focus on, it helps you balance.

Maintain the breath and put your right foot forward, knee slightly bent, with your left leg back and your left foot at an angle. Do not line up the feet as you would on railroad tracks, as you must allow some space for balance.

Your legs are your foundation. Think back to the last two yoga poses, Mountain and Tree, to find your ground. Root yourself. Now turn your hips straight ahead. Think of headlights on a car, blazing the way forward. Your hips are the headlights. With your upper body facing forward, raise your open arms above your head.

When you hold this pose, you are strong because you are rooted in the earth. You are a warrior in the spiritual sense.

Think of Athena, the goddess of wisdom who also maintained a warrior aspect. When her owl was spotted on the battlefield, warriors took it as a good omen.

This Warrior Pose expresses balance by building on the grounding of the first two poses and using that foundation to assume the Manipura stance of brave autonomy.

You can feel the earth below while you can grasp the energy above with your open hands. You are building a bridge from the Time Before the pandemic to the Time After the pandemic. You are tapping into the energetic flow of courage.

THE MEDITATION

Make yourself comfortable on your yoga mat because we are going to journey. Maybe lie down, and make sure you are warm enough.

Put your hand on your solar plexus. We are going to activate the Manipura chakra to make your courage flow. Engage your prana breath.

Breathe deeply into your solar plexus. In and out, slow and deep.

Can you see what is in there? What fear are you storing in your solar plexus?

Ask your solar plexus what it is holding onto, and imagine the Manipura chakra opening up.

Give it all the time it needs.

Breathe.

What do you see? What shape is it?

What do you feel?

Do you remember something from a long time ago?

Stay solid on your mat and let your soul do the work.

You may be remembering something recent, something from childhood, or something from another time and life.

Whatever you see, recognize the fear.

It is yours.

Own it.

Your Manipura chakra is opening and releasing the shape you see there.

Let it move through and out.

Now envision something you want very much but have been afraid to try or do or ask for.

See it.

Have the shapes changed?

What shape do you see now?

Send that shape into Manipura with your breath.

Fill the Manipura with a new shape.

The fear is gone.

What you want is there.

You have what you need to be your most courageous self.

Keep the shape with you as you come back to your mat and slowly return with your courage fully intact. You are strong and whole and enough.

You have the tools you need.

Writing Prompts

- What is your greatest fear?

- Has fear saved your life?

- Make a list of all the things you fear.

- How do you feel when you are frightened?

- How has fear held you back?

- How can you transmute the energy of fear into the energy of change?

OWL TALES

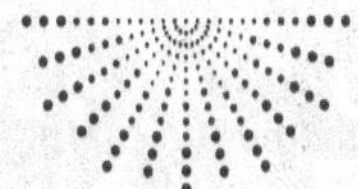

PLANT THE SEEDS OF FUTURE GROWTH

Persephone

Persephone picks
a handful of flowers
from a warm spring field
and seeks their seeds within.

Persephone travels,
willingly or not,
with Hades deep below the earth,
owl-led each year
to the place where seeds are born.

And so Persephone finds the seeds of one potential:
ice caps melting, tides flooding,
refugees moving, oceans choked with plastic,
animals dying, a dying planet,
pandemic.

And travels owl-led
ever deeper into the underworld
seeking seeds for a better potential,

and in the darkest underworld
she finds a ripened pomegranate,
the Ur seed of new beginnings
from earth's deep womb,
bursting with the smallest
red seeds of potential
ready to sprout.

OWL SEASONS

As nocturnal predators, owls are linked with the feminine, night, the moon, death, magic, and dreams.[1]

What do you see when you think of owls? The wise prophetic sage or the harbinger of doom and familiar of witches? Owls know many seasons and have appeared in many guises to different cultures over time.

The earliest artistic depiction of an owl is the long-eared owl painted in France's Chauvet Cave. Tools made of owl bones have also been found in ancient caves. Marija Gimbutas takes owls back the furthest, to Prehistoric Old Europe, as the bird goddesses seen in ancient carvings or the bas relief of Lilitu, which visually links goddess, woman, and bird.

In the ancient world, Greece and Rome appreciate Owl's wisdom as companion to Athena and Minerva, but Pliny associates owls with funerals, and Virgil tells us an owl's death howl from the temple's top foretold Dido's death.

William Shakespeare attributes these words to Richard III upon his receiving bad news: *"Out on you, owls! nothing but songs of death?"*

Surviving Native American owl lore preserves ancient owl traditions, describing the birds variously as trainers of shaman, guardians of the spirit world, and announcers of death.

According to Buddhist, Hindu, Jewish, and Christian traditions, owls are associated with witches and demonic forces.

Owls receive a mixed bag of reviews indeed, but their association with wisdom and the dark, prophecy, witchcraft, and the feminine, are what serves us best here and now.

PERSEPHONE, THE SEEDS, AND THE OWL

In Greek myth, Hades, the king of the underworld, kidnapped Persephone and brought her to his realm as the unwilling queen of the dead, where she was not to eat any food, to ensure she could return to her mother above. Everything was fine until she was seen by Ascalaphus, the guardian of Hades, eating the seed of a pomegranate.

Ascalaphus told the other gods Persephone had eaten the seed, and because of this, she had to stay with Hades in the underworld.

Persephone's mother, Demeter, was a powerful goddess, the Earth Mother from whom all life sprang. Hearing her daughter scream as Hades took her, Demeter searched unceasingly to find her. When she could not restore her daughter, Demeter was so angry she cursed all life from the land, and the seeds lay fallow, and winter fell while Persephone stayed with Hades in the underworld because she had eaten of the pomegranate.

Persephone was so angry, she turned Ascalaphus into an owl. According to Ovid:

> *...he became the vilest bird; a messenger of grief; the lazy owl; sad omen to mankind.*[2]

Really? In the end, Demeter enlists the help of other gods, including Helios, the god of the sun, to work out a compromise with Hades to return Persephone. Since Persephone had only eaten one pomegranate seed, it was agreed she could return to her mother and the earth's surface for half the year. So every spring Persephone comes back, bearing the seeds of potential, and life returns, as the sun warms the soil, and the seeds grow to maturity.

Let's look at this through owl eyes

Sylvia Brinton Perera, author of *Descent to the Goddess: A Way of Initiation for Women*, expresses the symbolism of the journey Persephone took, and which we must also take as women to incubate the seeds, to become whole, and once whole, to be able to build a world which reflects that wholeness:

> *The inner connection with the Goddess is an initiation essential for most modern women in the Western world; without it we are not whole. The process requires both a sacrifice of our identity as spiritual daughters of the patriarchy and a descent into the spirit of the Goddess, because so much power and passion of the feminine has been dormant in the Underworld—in exile for five thousand years.*

The story of Persophone is about bringing back the feminine power that resides in each of us and is about sowing the seeds of potential for the future. Having a wise owl around while you do that looks like a good idea.

The idea of cultivating potential leads us to our next Universal Law:

The Universal Law of Potential: The potential for anything is real. Manifest your best outcome by choosing the seeds that serve you and nurturing them carefully.

In other words, what you focus on will flourish: as the seeds of potential lie within the earth waiting for spring, they also lie within each of us waiting to grow.

Persephone goes underground during the coldest part of the year as life retreats from the earth for the winter and lies dormant. Remember the pomegranate seed. When Persephone returns to the surface in spring, the seeds grow, and new life is possible.

We are not much different in our quiet times, especially during the time of pandemic as we stay home to keep others safe. We are incubating the future, Persephone-like, anytime we wait, envision, and create. New life, or art, or new paradigms are all possible creations, in pandemic times or after, as we emerge with innovation, just as Persephone emerges from the underworld bringing spring.

As this pandemic time passes, how will we emerge? As we cross the bridge from the Time Before to the Time After, what will we create?

WHAT IS THE POTENTIAL OF THIS TIME BETWEEN TIMES?

Any time of waiting, of incubating the future in your mind, on your couch, or in the underworld, is about allowing the space for regeneration. Imagine the circle of life: from darkness comes light, from death comes life, from the seed comes growth.

LET'S LOOK THROUGH OWL EYES TO RETELL THE BIT ABOUT THE OWL

Persephone realizes the wisdom of the owl is crucial to all the potential coming from Hades each spring, and so she changes the guardian of Hades into a wise creature. Wisdom is also crucial to all the potential coming from us, and we, too, can call in owl magic when we need it to launch new projects and ideas and pursue new plans.

PRACTICING POTENTIAL IN CHALLENGING TIMES

Potential is the nugget that ripens, often in its own time. Incubation is one key, and time is another. Have you noticed that when you were little, summer seemed endless, and now it is over in the blink of an eye? The passage of time is malleable, as are the reasons for its passage.

We are probably all familiar with these lines from Ecclesiastes 3:1-8:

> *To every thing, there is a season,*
>
> *and a time to every purpose under the heaven:*
>
> *A time to be born, a time to die;*
>
> *a time to plant, and a time to pluck up that which is planted;*
>
> *A time to kill, and a time to heal;*
>
> *a time to break down, and a time to build up;*
>
> *A time to weep, and a time to laugh;*
>
> *a time to mourn, and a time to dance;*

A time to cast away stones, and a time to gather stones together;

a time to embrace, and a time to refrain from embracing;

A time to get, and a time to lose;

a time to keep, and a time to cast away;

A time to rend, and a time to sew;

a time to keep silence, and a time to speak;

A time to love, and a time to hate;

A time of war, and a time of peace.

What is the time we are living through now?

Ecclesiastes has seen it all. Each of the times mentioned has happened over and over again. We are not the first, and each of the times holds a powerful secret seed of potential we can draw from today as we create the future.

Let's break it down with owl vision

A time to be born, a time to die: In this Time Between, a new world is being born as everything we know is changing quickly. At the same time, death seems closer than it was in the Time Before. People are dying, and the old world order is dying.

A time to plant, and a time to pluck up that which is planted: Plant your seeds now, in the Time Between. These seeds are the plants we will pluck in the Time After. Plant wisely.

A time to kill, and a time to heal: A time to kill in the figurative sense, as in kill what isn't working, for you personally, and in the wider sense. We could 'kill' big oil, racism, and rogue capitalism, for example. At the same time, the Time Between is a time of healing, and 'killing' the bad provides room for the good to grow. Think of the planet breathing air suddenly fresh, water running clear, and animals appearing in now-empty urban places.

A time to break down, and a time to build up: The Time Between is our chance to break down what no longer serves, and build up what does serve for the Time After.

A time to weep, and a time to laugh: Let the tears flow. But remember the laughter, too. Spring will return.

A time to mourn, and a time to dance: We are facing a period of unprecedented collective grief. Let it move through you. Dance your grief now, that you may later dance your joy.

A time to cast away stones, and a time to gather stones together: Cast away everything that has failed—from personal habits to outdated systems. Gather the stones that work.

A time to embrace, and a time to refrain from embracing: The Time Between is the time of social distancing until a vaccine is found. It is a time to refrain from embracing, sadly, at the time we most want to be together. It will pass in its own time, with a vaccine or herd immunity.

A time to get, and a time to lose: We are getting something completely new much faster than we ever imagined. We are losing the old just as quickly.

A time to keep, and a time to cast away: The repeated theme of keeping what works and casting away what does not work is how we rebuild.

A time to rend, and a time to sew: Again, in the Time Between, rip it apart if it doesn't work, and sew it back together so it will work.

A time to keep silence, and a time to speak: The silence is the incubation of the seed. When you're ready, sing it from the rooftops!

A time to love, and a time to hate: There is plenty of hate in the world, but hate does not serve us. So cast it away, and replace it with love.

A time of war, and a time of peace: The Time Between is being called a time of war. Are we at war with a virus? The peace we need is always within, bring that peace out and help raise the collective to a place of peace.

THE YOGA POSE: BRIDGE POSE

We embody, quite literally, the bridge between two eras: the Time Before the pandemic and social unrest and the Time After the pandemic and social unrest. We are the bridge, and this is our pose.

To glean the full energetic benefits of Bridge Pose, use your prana breath.

Lie on your yoga mat and engage the breath. In and out. Deep breaths. Clear your mind.

Once you are settled, bend your knees and place your feet at hip's length before you.

Anchor your feet, take a very deep breath and slowly lift your hips from the floor keeping your knees apart at hip length.

You are activating the Mulahadra chakra to open your creativity.

Reach for your heels with your hands as you exhale.

Roll your arms under your shoulders to clasp our hands behind your back and lift up.

Support yourself through your legs and your solar plexus. You are opening the Anahata, your heart chakra.

Breathe deeply. Imagine the bridge and the connection you form between times.

Slowly lower yourself down.

THE MEDITATION

Settle comfortably on your yoga mat. You might lie down as you did to begin Bridge Pose, with your back flat and your knees bent.

Activate your prana breath, in and out, deep and slow.

Direct your awareness to the earth beneath you.

Lay your hands flat at your sides and let your fingers probe the earth's depth.

Let your toes reach deep into the earth, deeper and deeper.

Root yourself and travel deeper.

You're floating further and further down.

You feel like an autumn leaf, light on the breeze, drifting …

and finally, you settle gently.

You are floating in the deep center of the earth.

It is warm, and time has fallen away.

Every construct you know has fallen away.

You begin to hear a steady beating sound, and it soothes you.

This is the sound of life, the beating of the Earth Mother's heart, beating at the center point of all creation.

It is dark, but you begin to make out tiny seeds floating in the air.

You understand these are the seeds of Her potential, and also the seeds of your potential, because you are of Her and She manifests through you.

You are the sacred chalice, body, and mind. You are the creator.

You float in the warmth of sudden understanding and realize she is offering you seeds.

As many as you need, because the seeds of Her potential are endless.

You choose three handfuls: one for yourself, one for your creations, and one for your community.

You are ready to return to the surface with your handfuls of potential.

You rise 100 feet... 200 feet... at 300 feet you lose count.

You float as a leaf on a breeze to finally land on your yoga mat.

Your hands are full of seeds. You are ready to plant them, tend them, and realize their and your potential.

Writing Prompts

- What does potential mean to you?

- Where do you find your seeds?

- Describe your embodiment of the creative principle.

- If you met the Earth Mother, what would you tell her?

- Describe the seasons you are now living through.

7

MAGIC, MYTH AND YOGA

BECOME THE HERO OF YOUR STORY

Moon

The Streetlights
shone like moons
and she wanted them
all for herself.

IN THE BEGINNING, THERE WAS MAGIC

What are your earliest memories? Think back. For most of us, when we were small, the world was enchanted, and we were a part of its flow because everything the adult world declares inanimate is alive to the child.

CHILDHOOD IS MYTHIC, MAGIC, AND ALIVE

Mythologist Joseph Campbell talks about the absolute rapture of living, and he gives it a handle for us to grasp: Myth.

Myths are clues to the spiritual potentialities of human life.[1]

Campbell is concerned with the universal stories told by us all, which form the stories behind our personal story.

Remember your childhood stories? It is magic children understand, and it is something we can reclaim, remember, and retell through yoga and the heroic quest to integrate the universal laws we have practiced and the journeys we have taken so far. It leads to the crucial balance within ourselves between feminine and masculine as we reclaim our power to create and renew ourselves and the wider collective.

CALL IN YOUR OWLS

Yoga

Our yoga mats can take us anywhere we need to go. Yoga meditation breaks down the structures imposed by the adult world that took away childhood magic.

It is through yoga that we can access the mythic inner world of the universal consciousness. Here is where we can find our stories.

To get the most out of your story, apply the Law of Potential.

More from Joseph Campbell:

The images of myth are reflections of spiritual and depth potentialities of every one of us. Through contemplating those we evoke those powers in our own lives to operate through ourselves.[2]

Next, let's apply the Law of Detachment: Simply allow people and things to be as they are. Drop expectations and embrace the uncertainty. This will propel you forward.

WHAT WE ARE MISSING TODAY IS MYTHOLOGY AND POETRY

We are disconnected from our stories because the structures of the adult world value material profit, and in the pursuit of profit, we forget our inner journeys as we grow up and conform to those structures. If we drop the expectations and embrace detachment, we can move beyond the structures.

BECOME THE HERO OF YOUR OWN STORY

Every story has a hero, and you are the hero of your own story. You already carry every myth you need within yourself. We all do.

From the Upanishads of India:

Heaven, hell, and all the gods are within us.

We need to remember the rapture of being alive.

OPEN YOUR OWL EYES TO LOOK THROUGH AND BEYOND

Campbell tells us it is really about the experience of life and what can be named:

See life like a poem, you are participating in a poem, and the root of the poetry is myth.[3]

When a society forgets its stories or its old stories fail to work, it forgets how to live and enters free fall. We see this historically in societies colonized by the west, and we see it today in our society.

A lack of story leads to an attraction to extremes in religion, politics, and civic life, including dangerous fundamentalism. Look no further than the evening news.

It is about retelling your stories.

People living without myth must find their own mythology. Start by opening your heart and your mind to the mystery of it all. Grow awareness of the mystery in all things, including yourself.

You can remember this from your earliest childhood.

The theme of the goddess as the earth runs through Campbell's work, and he is clear that remembering the feminine principles, including life and nurture, with the liberation of the feminine from the old patriarchal construct of only mother, will do much to help us re-cherish the earth.

> In the older view the goddess Universe was alive, herself organically the Earth, the horizon, and the heavens. Now she is dead, and the universe is not an organism, but a building, with gods at rest in it in luxury: not as personifications of the energies in their manners of operation, but as luxury tenants, requiring service. And Man, accordingly, is not as a child born to flower in the knowledge of his own eternal portion but as a robot fashioned to serve.[4]

Re-enchanting the earth by bringing back the sacred feminine so we re-cherish women and the earth is revolutionary thinking. It means re-imagining the Earth as a living being while liberating humanity from empty service to empty gods to flower to its full potential.

The Heroine's Journey

Let your owls guide you.

Maureen Murdock, a Jungian psychotherapist and student of Joseph Campbell, enlarged upon the idea of the hero's journey in her book *The Heroine's Journey: Woman's Quest for Wholeness*[5] to create a template of Campbell's well known *Hero's Journey* that women can use.

Murdock elaborates upon Campbell's idea of re-enchanting the feminine principle, and thus the earth, as she presents the heroine's journey as the healing of the wounded feminine that exists deep within individual women and deep within the larger culture.

> *The feminine journey is about going down deep into soul, healing, and reclaiming, while the masculine journey is up and out, to spirit.*[6]

The heroine's journey is about reclaiming the feminine and integrating it with the masculine to achieve the balance that brings peace to the individual and through the individual to the collective. It's an eight-step journey available to all of us.

Taking the Heroine's Journey in Challenging Times

There is a connection between the way we treat the earth and the way we treat women: when we degrade women, it translates into degrading the earth and vice versa, forming a vicious circle that leaves women and our culture separated from the feminine aspect. Murdock's Heroine's Journey is about reclaiming the feminine, and the eight stages she provides can be used in any order you need.

Each stage of the heroine's journey involves the transformation of energy from one thing to something else, which brings us to our next universal law:

The Law of Perpetual Transmutation of Energy: Everything, including us, is made of energy, and can alternate form between matter and energy, physical and spiritual, rendering us immortal. The transmutation of energy can help us create and re-create our own realities.

We can transmute ourselves, and when we do, we are transmuting the collective

The first stages of the heroine's journey cover separation of the individual from feminine attributes such as intuition, nurture, and creation in favor of the masculine values of the patriarchy.

It leads not to physical death, but to a death of the spirit, which leads to the middle part of the heroine's journey, the inward journey to reclaim the lost feminine.

In the final stages of the journey, the feminine principle is re-found and re-united with the masculine principle.

In a series of transmutations, the journey brings us back to our feminine self and re-balances us with the masculine.

The Heroine's Journey can occur many times throughout the life of one woman:

Adolescence, when a girl moves from childhood to womanhood; childbirth, when a woman becomes a mother; and menopause or old age.

Any major stage of life can become a Heroine's Journey, and it is possible that right now, many women are taking the journey in an instinctive effort to raise the collective consciousness.

As these women restore their own feminine principle, they are also restoring the lost feminine principles of the collective to help rebalance the world.

It is the same theme of descent and return we have been practicing all along.

This is the work of the Between Time that will help rebuild the post-pandemic world.

The following journey echoes the structure of the earlier journeys, but shifts the focus from the original individual level to the collective level. We can undertake this new, broader collective journey now to reintegrate the feminine aspect in our lives and culture to help move ourselves and our society forward.

THE COLLECTIVE JOURNEY TO REINTEGRATE THE FEMININE ASPECT IN THE PANDEMIC AGE

Rejection of the feminine principle

Modern patriarchal society has rejected the feminine principle. Women and the earth are abused, the life-giving principle is forgotten, and the imbalance leads to global problems such as climate change and pandemic.

Embracing of the masculine principle

Modern patriarchal society has embraced power and control to an extent that it is detrimental to life on this planet.

The challenge

Western civilization has been lauded as the end of history, the best outcome civilization could reach, when in fact it is impermanent and—in its rejection of the feminine life force—riddled with the seeds of its own undoing.

The illusion of success

Society has overcome many past challenges, but it has done so by suppressing the feminine aspect it needs to survive. That is the emptiness many are trying now to fill.

Descending to meet the goddess

Society is now beset by crisis in the form of pandemic. The continuing of yesterday's habits, all based on a patriarchal framework of destruction for profit, will fail us as solutions. We must collectively return to the feminine life force, and as we make that shift, we meet the goddess and strive to return to femininity. That is why we see such an upsurge of witchcraft with so many opportunities to connect in circles right now.

Reconnection to the feminine

Within patriarchy, people yearn to reinstate the missing feminine. They may turn to the goddess or the land, but will find the old ways of doing that predate patriarchy are no longer working.

Balance with the masculine

Patriarchy continues in crisis, and, in its search for a solution, begins to heal the negative masculine and embrace the positive masculine. This is a strength and protection.

Bringing it together

Society moves forward in a new balance of feminine and masculine, which restores and protects the creative life principle to allow life to flourish.

THE YOGA POSE: GODDESS POSE

Assimilate the Heroine's Journey with Goddess Pose.

Assuming Goddess Pose is something we can do at any time to draw upon our strength and to lend strength to others. In all her guises, the powerful energy of the goddess, of the earth, of life, is there. She gives freely, and she has never been fully eclipsed because she is an integral part of the whole.

Our yoga mats do not return us to a mythical time in prehistory. They allow us to reconnect to an ancient aspect of ourselves that offers the crucial balance we need to bring forward to rebalance the present.

On your yoga mat, or if you can, outside with bare feet to really connect to the earth, stand tall with your legs bent and your feet pointing out. Raise your arms like goal posts, hands up with palms facing forward. Stand straight and strong from the torso while grounding the legs.

This is the yoga pose of the goddess.

THE MEDITATION

Get comfortable on your yoga mat.

Breathe into your heart chakra.

Imagine you are walking out the door into the woods.

You are seeking life and all its manifestations.

You meet a beautiful doe, and she leads you.

Deeper into the forest.

The path leads through trees and fields.

You recognize many friends, they are the living creatures of the woods.

Life abounds under the canopy of trees.

The doe leads you to a tree, and nestled in the tree is an alter showing an ancient female form. She is surrounded by offerings. You add your own offering, a special stone you carry in your pocket.

The sunlight dapples through the trees, and you see something there, something light and very much alive.

The doe has been joined by an owl and transformed into pure light.

The light envelopes you, warming you, and you are unquestionably alive at that moment. You are given a view of the past, the future, and you see yourself straddling the two and building the new world to come.

You embody, for a moment, the life force. Its power emanates from you to the world.

When the light has faded, the doe resumes her former shape and leads you back along the trail in the woods. The doe returns you gently to your yoga mat, and you bring the power of creation with you.

Writing Prompts

- What old constructs are you clinging to?

- How can you re-myth your stories?

- Write about your childhood magic.

- When have you embodied the goddess?

- Imagine ways the collective can re-myth the world.

- Describe what the cherishing of nature and women look like in practice?

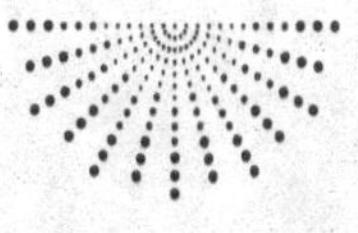

8
WATER MAGIC

RENEWAL

Beyond

Out beyond ideas of wrongdoing
and rightdoing there is a field.
I'll meet you there. ~Rumi

THE TRANSFORMATIVE POWER OF WATER

The ocean is always the same yet different. High tide, low tide, calm or storm, the ocean transforms itself endlessly. Science and myth converge in asserting the first life arose from the water, the primeval soup, in a process reenacted in every womb to this day. More than half of the adult human body is water, and 71% of the planet is covered by oceans.

How many times have you received your Eureka! moment floating in the bathtub or swimming in the sea?

The places where water meets the land are powerful liminal spaces marking the lines of energy between earth and water. Between the two is an enchanted spot, and if you walk along it, you can see the transformative power of the water. Notice perhaps the rocks, and how the water has carved its way through them. Notice the creeks, where water determines the shape and depth of the marsh. Watch a storm come in on a high moon tide, and see entire chunks of land blown away as the landscape transforms over and over again.

Water always knows its level, and water always knows how to fill a space. It is pretty much unstoppable.

Water is working with a specific universal law:

The Universal Law of Least Effort: Accept things as they are.

> *Today I will accept people, situations, circumstances, and events as they occur. I will know that this moment is as it should be, because the whole universe is as it should be. I will not struggle against the whole universe by struggling against this moment. My acceptance is total and complete. I accept things as they are at this moment, not as I wish they were.*[1]

Water is acting within the scope of how things are, and there is no need for struggle within its magic power of transformation. Water transforms coastlines because that is the nature of water. You also embody transformation naturally.

Every November on the beaches of Cape Cod, people wait for the return of the migratory Snowy Owl. We do not have a record of what the local Natives thought about Snowy Owl, but other Native traditions from off-Cape associate Snowy Owl with medicine, which points to a healing component.

An association with Snowy Owl helps you dig into the deepest part of your nature, the light and dark, and when you dig into the dark, you can become, owl-like, the shapeshifter with all-seeing eyes. Snowy Owl helps you look inward to remember old knowledge, with heightened night vision.

These are things that simply are, and our owl eyes can help us see them clearly.

As we search within, we transform ourselves, and as we transform ourselves, we transform society. While that is the overriding message of this Time Between, the middle point of the pandemic and political crisis, it will hold its value long after this stage has passed as we continue to rebuild and redefine everything.

We are individually and collectively digging out the cold winter dark parts so we can transform them into something better.

It helps to combine Snowy Owl with the ocean and the moon to make exceptionally powerful magic.

Another valuable tool is recalling all the previous laws and journeys we have encountered so far:

Remember the Law of Connection, to pull this all together, the Law of Detachment to embrace uncertainty, and the Law of Least Effort when you must accept things as they are. Remember the Law of Attraction, because like always attracts like, and the Law of Perpetual Transmutation of Energy, which allows constant creation. If you are frightened, call in the Law of Love and the Law of Courage to banish fear, and when you sense scarcity, the handmaid of fear, remember the Universal Law of Giving and Receiving, and most of all, remember to plant the seeds of the Law of Potential.

Bear the armor of these laws as you navigate the future.

We start by following the moon in her three aspects of maiden, mother, and crone.

She is the ultimate shapeshifter, going through three significant transformations a month as well as vanishing completely during the new moon phase.

The seeds of potential lie waiting in the dark of the moon, and from them the moon grows full. This is personified by the maiden.

As the moon reaches fullness, it personifies the mother, full and fecund, and at the height of her powers blossoming like the spring. She is the creator, not necessarily of life, but of many things, such as art, poetry, or plants, anything she chooses. She is clothed in the springtime.

Finally, the moon wanes, and the sky darkens. This stage is personified by the crone's ancient wisdom. She is associated with winter, the season of Snowy Owl. Call upon her to look through and beyond.

The owl rides the winds of change as the moon directs the tidal waters in and out in perpetual renewal.

It is an endless cycle, and we are going to tap into it with our owl eyes wide open.

THE YOGA POSE AND MEDITATION: SAVASANA

In the last chapter, we went on an all-out Heroine's Journey. This time, through Savasana, we will reflect on that same journey as it comes up at the end of each yoga sequence in a more simple way.

To consolidate the wisdom we have gathered, let's combine the pose with the meditation.

Get comfortable on your yoga mat, lie flat and loose.

Savasana is a Sanskrit word, forming a compound of the words *shava*, which means death, and *asana*, which means posture. The two words joined together translate to corpse pose.

Savasana is simply lying still upon your mat. It is a yoga session's final powerful pose and can be hard to define as an experience.

It is a voyage of transformation, and it is something that happens as we simply allow it.

Focus your owl eyes to see through and beyond. We are gathering the wisdom received to bring back to rebuild in the Time Between and the Time After.

You are confident and prepared for the future.

In Savasana, remember the phases of the moon and the power of the tides, and imagine the Snowy Owl riding the cold wind over the shoreline.

Become the Snowy Owl. What do you see?

Align your body with both the earth and the cosmos. Create a balance between the two, far beyond the dualities of the mundane world.

Become the water flowing unimpeded, you find the level of your intuition, the place where dualities are simply aspects of the same thing and thus not contentious.

Remain bodily rooted to your mat, while internally riding the flow.

Imagine the flow as the conduit, as electricity travels the wire to light the lamp, we can travel the flow to self-realization and the greater consciousness.

Here is the Eureka! moment. Gather your wisdom.

Ride Savasana back to the Heroine's Journey whenever you need to with these simple steps:

Assemble your tools, the Universal Laws, the owl wings and vision, and accept the mission, which you have done by simple virtue of stepping onto the mat.

Embark upon the quest by setting a specific intention and enter the flow. You will encounter extraordinary places and experiences outside of the work-a-day world.

Allow it.

Realize the set intention through the flow, and take time to assimilate the knowledge thus gained.

You may sojourn for a spell in the underworld or through the heavens, and for all practical purposes appear to be dead. A yogi reclining in Savasana appears lifeless.

But like Persephone awaiting summer, you are merely resting, assimilating the body of knowledge gained upon the journey, and preparing to bring the knowledge back to the work-a-day world.

Savasana culminates the journey

Yoga is a Sanskrit word and means to yoke with the divine. When we enter the flow, we open the door to that joining, and the possibilities are endless.

This is what Julian of Norwich did with Body Prayer.

Savasana returns us from the quest of the flow, allowing us to integrate the experience of the journey from the mat to the regular world.

We need only look, and, beautifully, once seen, the wisdom stays with us, and we can share it far and wide in this new world we must create as we navigate these Between Times.

Writing Prompts

- Describe your meditation.

- What have you brought back from meditation?

- Write a letter to the future about your hope.

- What is your wisdom?

- How can you share your wisdom with others?

CHAKRA GUIDE AND PRANA

1. **Sahasrara**, the Thousandfold Chakra. At the crown of the head. Color: white. Consciousness and connection to the third eye. Sahasrara brings cosmic understanding to remind us of divine unity.

2. **Ajna**, the Chakra of Light. The pineal gland in the brow between the eyes. Color: blue to indigo. The third eye, home of insight and intuition. You can see blue and indigo floating behind closed eyelids when your third eye activates.

3. **Vishuddha**, the Sound Chakra. The throat. Color: blue. Sound, including speech and communication, an important means of connection.

4. **Anahata**, the Heart Chakra. The heart. Color: green. Yin and yang, the union of opposites, male and female, balance and love.

5. **Manipura**, the Fire Chakra. The solar plexus. Color: yellow. The sun and the fire that sustains life and growth.

6. **Swadhisthana**, the Chakra of Pleasure. The stomach, the womb, and the reproductive organs. Color: orange. Water and creation.

7. **Muladhara**, the Root Chakra. The perineum. Color: red. The lowest chakra is dense with the secretions of birth and life. Connects us to the earth.

Prana: *Hinduism: a life-breath or vital principle in Vedic and later Hindu religion* ~ Merriam Webster Dictionary

NOTES

6. OWL TALES

1. Werness, Hope B., (2006) *The Continuum, Encyclopedia of Animal Symbolism in Art*, p. 303
2. Ovid Metamorphoses, Book V

7. MAGIC, MYTH AND YOGA

1. Campbell, Joseph, with Bill Moyers, (1991) *The Power of Myth*
2. *Ibid.*
3. Campbell, Joseph, and Bill Moyers (1988) from Ep. 2: Joseph Campbell and the Power of Myth — 'The Message of the Myth'
4. Campbell, Joseph, (2013) *Goddesses: Mysteries of the Feminine Divine*, xxii
5. Murdock, Maureen, (1990) *The Heroine's Journey: Woman's Quest for Wholeness*
6. Davis, Mary (2005). "Maureen Murdock" (PDF). *Jung Society of Atlanta*. Retrieved 2019-04-02.

8. WATER MAGIC

1. Chopra, Deepak, (1994) *The Seven Spiritual Laws of Success*

ACKNOWLEDGMENTS

Owl Magic is the result of a wonderful series of collaborations. Small-press publishing does not happen in a vacuum. It takes an excited and dedicated team. I had the text, but it needed to go through the polishing process that makes a book. So I looked around and noticed I was surrounded by creativity. My deepest thanks to the following editors, artists, and writers who helped take *Owl Magic* from manuscript to book:

Eugenia Petrovits Nordskog, for unfailing support and the kind of thorough editing that makes books truly readable.

Rikke Dakin Photography, for very generously providing the cover image from the beautiful Belgian forest collection.

Sybil Wilson at Popkitty Design for capturing the cover exactly.

And the outstanding team of beta-readers, for providing crucial feedback as we pulled it all together.

October 2020,

Naarden

ABOUT THE AUTHOR

Mary Petiet is an author, poet, and freelance writer. She is the author of *Minerva's Owls* and *Moon Tide: Cape Cod Poems*. In 2020 she founded Sea Crow Press, a small independent imprint curating creative nonfiction and poetry to give her titles a home.

Mary writes with a passion for connecting and empowering women to live from their highest selves. She is a contributor to the anthologies *Jesus, Muhammad, and the Goddess, She Rises, vol.2,* and *Awaken the Feminine!: Dismantling Domination to Restore Balance on Mother Earth*. Her work has appeared in *Feminism and Religion, Sage Woman, The Wayfarer*, and she is a contributor to *Mother House of the Goddess*. Mary is a graduate of the University of St Andrews.

Join Mary on Facebook or online at www.marypetiet.com and be the first to hear about her new books. She loves to hear from readers at marypetiet@gmail.com and is available for work with book groups and online readings. If you love *Owl Magic*, please be sure to tell your friends and leave a review on Amazon and Good Reads.

SEA CROW PRESS

COMMITTED TO BUILDING AN ACCESSIBLE COMMUNITY OF WRITERS, DEDICATED TO TELLING STORIES THAT MATTER

Sea Crow Press is named for a flock of five talkative crows you can find on the beach anywhere between Scudder Lane and Bone Hill Road in Barnstable Village on Cape Cod.

According to Norse legend, one-eyed Odin sent two crows out into the world so they could return and tell its stories. If you sit and listen to the sea crows in Barnstable as they fly and roost and chatter, it's an easy legend to believe.

Sea Crow Press is dedicated to telling stories that matter, and *Owl Magic: Your Guide to Challenging Times* is a gift for everyone navigating the challenges of today's quickly shifting landscape.